Through All of It

A Daughter's Story:
Navigating the Dementia Journey with Her Mom and Dad

Peggy Masterson

ISBN 979-8-88851-102-2 (Paperback)
ISBN 979-8-88851-103-9 (Digital)

Covenant Books
11661 Hwy 707
Murrells Inlet, SC 29576
www.covenantbooks.com

Through All of It was written for you… and for every
family dealing with a dementia diagnosis.

It has been inspired by my loving parents, Clara and Jim
Cullinan, who took me on my first life-changing dementia journey,
and all the amazing seniors and their families that have crossed my
path ever since.

Contents

Acknowledgments vii

Introduction ix

Some Added Encouragement: My Playlist xi

1   An Ordinary Life 1

2   The Signs 3

3   The Cover-Up 6

4   On the Road 10

5   The First Few Swings 13

6   Being the Punching Bag 17

7   Now I'm Scared...20

8   Everybody's Angry 22

9   Taking Its Toll...25

10   The Fall 27

11   The Storm 30

12   The Tsunami..33

13   No More Choices 36

14   Shopping for Assisted Living 39

15   The Move...40

16   Time To Liquidate 46

17   The Estate Sale 48

18   Losing Dad 51

19   At Home with Mom...53

20   Memory Care 55

21   Hip No. 2 58

22   Finally Home 61

Lessons Learned 65

A Few Final Thoughts..75

Acknowledgments

I would never have had the courage to set out on the adventure of writing this book if it wasn't for the unending encouragement from my husband and children. Thank you, Bill, Kaitlyn, and Connor, for believing that the energy and effort tied to writing this book will make a difference to others. You are my rocks and my best friends.

I am also grateful for my personal experiences with dementia. Although many were painful and unpleasant, they have been the source of my commitment to assist others as they face this challenge. Without their impact on my life, I would have nothing credible to draw from to provide encouragement.

Our heavenly Father tells us that everything we experience in this lifetime has a purpose that only He knows and understands. Each of these experiences is designed to teach us something and ultimately strengthen our faith in Him. We are also directed to share our experiences with other believers in an effort to encourage and/or comfort them in the midst of their struggles. This story is shared with you to strengthen you in what can be some of your darkest moments with a loved one. I tell it so you will know that you are never alone in this journey and to encourage you to lean on others as well as your faith. It is too difficult to do alone.

This journey with dementia (*my story in the pages that follow*) changed the trajectory of my life. I left a multiyear career in the corporate world to pursue a second career in senior care. I am currently 100 percent focused on serving seniors, their families, and their care providers by delivering quality dementia education and training.

I am a nationally certified dementia trainer (NCCDP), a licensed executive director for both assisted living and memory care facilities, and I have my own dementia training company called Dealing with

Dementia. (dealingwdementia.com). It is my prayer that those dealing with dementia, in any way, shape, or form, can easily access the support, training, and education that they need to cope with this devasting diagnosis.

Introduction

I am just like you. I'm a daughter, wife, cousin, mom, and hardworking professional. I am an only child that was faced with a double whammy of dementia when *both* of my parents began to exhibit signs of early onset dementia when I was in my forties *(probably sooner if I was paying closer attention)*.

I was in the midst of my first career at the time that my parents' health began to decline, and I was also busy raising a family of my own. I was no longer living in my hometown, so I was trying to manage their decline from several states away. I watched as things got progressively worse at home. The flights back home got more frequent and lasted longer each time. I tried everything I could think of to get them the help I knew they needed, but the best I could accomplish was a friendly neighbor that was willing to keep an eye on them in my absence. They adamantly declined any and all other alternatives *(sound familiar?)*.

My story is the foundation of what has now become my passion in the second half of my professional life. This series of events and experiences opened my eyes to a need that has been greatly underserved. Families need to be informed, supported, and guided through the challenges of caring for their senior loved one. Sharing my story with you is the first step of many I plan to take to do what I can to assist.

I believe that it is what we learn along the way that really matters in life. How we learn to cope with the numerous situations that will certainly present themselves, dictate our path, and serve to form our character.

It is amazing to realize how God works in each of our lives every day. Every situation I have found myself in and every person that crosses my path has been placed there "deliberately" and for a specific purpose. It has become clear that either I have something to learn from them or I have something to share with them. If you can view whatever life throws at you through this lens, I am certain you will prevail.

It is my prayer that our crossing paths today, you're picking up my story to read, will be one of those deliberate events that will inform, encourage, and benefit *you*.

Any illness diagnosis stops us in our tracks, but this "brain failure" is especially crippling because there is currently no cure or even a hopeful prognosis. When faced with any hardship, we have a choice to make. Will I allow myself to be defeated, or will I find ways to make the most of the time I have left with my loved one? I hope you choose to get the information, training, and insight that will give you the tools to allow you to make the most of every remaining moment.

Some Added Encouragement

My Playlist

If you are open to it, I would love this story to be an "experience" for you versus a simple book.

If you are like me, you probably love music. They say music is the universal language because it speaks to us on an emotional level. The rhythm and melody have the power to lift my soul regardless of whether I know the lyrics.

I have found Christian music to be an *incredible* source of strength and encouragement. I invite you to experience the same.

I have put together a playlist for you of some of the most uplifting Christian songs from several amazing artists. These musicians/songwriters are truly gifted, and I believe their gift to all of us should be shared.

I know you will enjoy the melodies, but if you are like me, you will probably grow to memorize all the lyrics too! Each of them has a powerful message to hear, and because I want you to be as encouraged as possible, I wanted to share them with you.

As you move through the pages that follow, you will find that I have sprinkled in a reference to these songs *(you will find them listed by number and name at many of the chapter breaks).*

The addition of Christian music is intended to be a small (unexpected) way to bless you. Be reminded, once again, that God is in everything. He is everywhere. He knows every tiny detail of your life. Let these songs remind you that what you are going through is part of His bigger plan for you, and He will never leave you unattended or unloved. He has given us the gifts of these musicians to be yet another way of reaching us and reminding us He is with us *through all of it*!

So let's get started. The theme song for this story is number 1 on the playlist below. "Through All of It" by Colton Dixon.

Start there and look for other playlist references as you read on. Perhaps I will see you singing your heart out at some stoplight one day! Be blessed and encouraged.

My Playlist

1. "Through All of It" by Colton Dixon
2. "God Is in This Story" by Katy Nichole and Big Daddy Weave
3. "The Prayer" by Danny Gokey and Natalie Grant
4. "Haven't Seen It Yet" by Danny Gokey
5. "You Raise Me Up" by Josh Groban
6. "I Know" by Big Daddy Weave
7. "Word of God Speak" by Mercy Me
8. "Famous For" by Tauren Wells
9. "Hold Me Jesus" by Big Daddy Weave
10. "God Speaking" by Mandisa
11. "You Are Loved" by Josh Groban
12. "Stand in Faith" by Danny Gokey
13. "The Other Side" by Colton Dixon
14. "Overcomer" by Mandisa
15. "God's Not Done with You" by Tauren Wells
16. "Tell Your Heart to Beat Again" by Danny Gokey

1

An Ordinary Life

No. 1 Through All of It by Colton Dixon

By all accounts, I have been blessed from my earliest days. I was adopted when I was six months old by two amazing people. I grew up as an only child in snowy Buffalo, New York. I never really wanted anything except for maybe an older brother to watch out for me or someone to play with now and then. As a modest middle-class couple, Mom and Dad sacrificed a great deal to send me to a private school. I took ballet *(which I was politely asked to discontinue because of my lack of ability),* tap dancing, gymnastics, skiing, swimming, tennis, ice skating, and essentially all the privileges a child could ask for.

I'll admit that I was afforded a lot of opportunities that would exceed the definition of ordinary life! Mom and Dad had their struggles now and then, but nobody is perfect. Discipline was hard, rules were abundant, and expectations were high, but I always knew I was loved.

I graduated from high school and left for college in Syracuse, New York. I think those initial days away from home were when I realized how much I missed my mom and dad. I would come home for all the college breaks and holidays and began to notice our relationship was evolving into a more adult friendship. I truly respected their advice and direction.

After I graduated from college, I came home and worked two to three jobs at a time before I landed my first *real* career role. This role required me to relocate for what turned out to be for good. I left home in my early twenties and never returned.

I called home every weekend and came home for all the holidays. My career advanced, I met my husband, and shortly thereafter, we had two amazing children. Life got busier, calls home got fewer, and although we still got together for the holidays, the visits got more hectic and stressful.

Mom and Dad made efforts to come to visit us as they realized it was a challenge traveling with small children. They even flew for the first time since WWII to travel to Cleveland, Ohio, for Christmas! This was an awesome time and one of my most treasured memories. I can still see Dad holding our infant son. He was so unsure of what to do with an infant, but his love for that little baby was beaming all over his face. That Christmas, Bill, my husband, and Mom stayed up until the wee hours of the morning assembling an electric jeep and arguing over how to assemble a cash register toy that Santa was bringing to the children. I can still see my dad holding our infant son as if he was afraid he would break. He smiled as I had never seen him smile that day. It's a memory I deeply treasure.

As time wore on, we got transferred to Alabama, which made the visits even more difficult. Mom and Dad still made the trip for a couple of Christmases, but we began to notice that the chaos of a household of young children would wear on their patience. Things became stressful, and tensions ran high. Initially, they would come for two weeks over the holidays, but over time, the length of their visits became shorter and shorter.

We got transferred a couple more times, and I recall noticing a distinct decline in both of their appearances when they arrived in Nashville, Tennessee, that Christmas. They had both aged physically since we had seen them last, but I simply attributed it to the aging process. This was when I first began to notice their decline. Dad had lost a great deal of weight, and Mom was repeating herself and asking the same questions several times over the course of the day. Again, I thought these were just normal signs of aging.

2

The Signs

No. 2 "God Is in This Story" by Katy Nichole and Big Daddy Weave

That year, the phone calls home began to get more challenging. Mom would not come to the phone very often (*unless dad forced her to*). The conversations became more difficult, and the questions more repetitive. There was never anything new or any of the wonderful stories they would tell about some adventure they encountered. They would ask about my husband, work, or the grandkids but would often forget their names or recall that they were in first grade when they were in third or fourth grade. The struggles of caring for their home were getting bigger *(shoveling the driveway, mowing the lawn, and raking the leaves)*. I would offer to get them some help, but of course, that was "completely ridiculous."

There is a big difference between what is called "normal aging" and the early symptoms of dementia. All of us will have those "senior moments" where we forget where we placed things, or we find ourselves staring at the pantry, wondering what we came in there looking for. The distinction, however, is that we can normally give it a few minutes, and we will recall whatever it is we are searching for. These instances will happen occasionally, and they will likely be harmless in the scheme of things.

The changes taking place with Mom and Dad were much more than normal aging, but I didn't know any better at the time. I grew increasingly worried about their well-being. Dad was the financial manager of the household and began missing payments on several of the household bills. Mom never missed a birthday or holiday for the grandkids and began forgetting key events that always meant the world to her. This is where my journey began as I started to make more solo flights back to Buffalo, New York, to check in on them.

It was Dad's eightieth birthday, and I decided to make a surprise trip to see how things were going at home. My parents were still living in the same home they had built back in 1960, but they were always meticulous about keeping it maintained. Mom was religious about the beautiful roses that stretched across the front of the modest ranch home. Dad was diligent about keeping a weed-free luscious-looking lawn. They often boasted about the neighborhood recognition they received for "lawn or the month" and assorted other accolades.

The cab pulled up to their home, and I could not believe my eyes. The lawn was un-mowed and full of dandelions, the flower beds were empty, and mom's roses were unruly and almost dead. I knew immediately that something was very wrong.

Dad was unshaven, wearing a dirty, coffee-stained T-shirt. He was sitting in his favorite folding chair with the garage door open when I came walking up the driveway. He was so excited to see me and quickly welcomed me with a big hug. As he called out to Mom to announce my arrival, I noticed his frail frame. He had probably lost about twenty pounds since I had seen him at Christmas.

Mom was delighted at my arrival but immediately went into the "worry mode," as I call it, worrying about what she would serve to eat (it's odd how you can be made to feel like a guest in the same home you grew up in as the year's pass). As much as I would try to convince her not to fuss, it was part of what brought her joy.

Mom was also an amazing cook. She could make the most out of anything, and it was always delicious. She was never one to allow me to assist much in the cooking process, so I sat at the kitchen table and chatted with her while she was preparing dinner. I noticed she went back and forth to the pantry and the refrigerator multiple times to try to assemble the ingredients she needed. After an unusually long process, she got everything in the oven, and we went to visit with Dad on the back porch.

As I walked through the house, it was clear the home had not been cleaned in months. Mom was also a "white glove" kind of housekeeper, so this was quite a shock to me. I'm certainly no one to judge, as I am no superstar housekeeper, but this was so unlike Mom. It was also odd that she didn't seem to notice the dust or stains on the carpet where Dad had spilled his coffee.

We visited for a short while, and Dad was consistently missing the table when he went to set down his drink. His vision and depth perception were clearly off. When he got up, I noticed his balance was shaky as well. I asked him what was going on, and he insisted it was just a little "bug" he was getting over.

Dinner was alarming that evening. The pork chops were so overcooked we couldn't even cut them, and the scalloped potatoes were almost raw. I ate applesauce that evening and went to bed in tears. I was so scared and afraid.

Once again, I never said anything about these changes. I tried but could not find the courage to openly discuss what I knew needed to be said. I left my childhood home with a heavy heart and returned to my home over one thousand miles away. My worry and anxiety over their decline were on my mind every day, all day.

3

The Cover-Up

No. 3 "The Prayer" by Danny Gokey and Natalie Grant

I'm sure I paid that bill. There's no way I'm paying a late fee. Did I take my pills today? How do I get back home? Someone stole my keys! Did I turn the stove off?

These instances of forgetfulness are now entering a more serious space that indicates a failure to safely manage things for themselves. These instances are likely happening more frequently and are initiating a sense of fear in individuals experiencing them. As a result of their fear, you will find that they will try to cover up their shortfalls.

We are all prideful beings, and none of us like to be exposed. Think about the last time you didn't know the answer to something or perhaps didn't know how to do something that everyone else thought you should know. What did you do? I know my first instinct is to do everything I possibly can to *not* look stupid. I might laugh or change the subject, but it is unlikely I will admit that I don't know something.

Our parents (or seniors) feel that same way. They know things are changing for them, but they definitely don't want us to know, thus begins the cover-up.

In my story, the initial cover-up was related to Dad's health. He was a WWII veteran and insisted on having all his healthcare managed through the veteran's administration. I noticed that Dad had been losing a considerable amount of weight over the course of my last few visits, so I began to ask him about his health. Of course, I was told he was just fine and that his doctor had everything under control. I could tell I was getting "stonewalled" regarding this issue, so I decided to track down his doctor myself to ask some questions. After numerous phone calls, I finally found her, only to learn that without a healthcare power of attorney, I was unable to learn anything further about his condition. I didn't even know what a healthcare power of attorney was at the time.

I spoke with Mom about my concerns about Dad's health, and she was just as uninformed as I was. I approached Dad about getting a healthcare power of attorney, and it was like I lit a set of fireworks under his living room recliner. He was furious that I would meddle in his affairs. He made it abundantly clear that this health was his business and no one else's. That was the first of many uncomfortable conversations.

As it turned out, Dad had experienced a series of ministrokes, and the most recent one had taken the vision in his right eye. This explained his balance and depth perception issues, but I never learned the truth until months later.

Dad knew his vision limitations would result in losing his license, so he covered it up. His judgment was clearly distorted. I knew it was only a matter of time before he would be in some sort of accident.

Mom's cover-up was less easily concealed. She asked the same questions over and over again, she'd run around in circles trying to find all the ingredients for a given recipe, her cooking was suddenly unfit to eat, and her denial about any shortcomings was healthier than anything else. Mom was always very active and an incredibly hard worker. As her dementia progressed, she refused to accept the fact that it may not be safe for her to do some of the things she had always done around the house.

My childhood home was built some fifty years earlier and had an open attic that could only be accessed from a ladder in the garage. That January, Mom decided to climb the ladder to place all the Christmas decorations in their attic storage spot. One of her legs slipped through the rungs in the ladder and resulted in a deep bruise and wound that ran the entire length of her shin. She never told Dad and certainly never told me.

Weeks went by while she chose to care for the wound on her own. The pain got continually worse until she finally told my dad what had happened. When the pain got to the point that Mom could not sleep at night, and she suspected it was infected, they finally went to the local urgent care clinic. The doctor took one look at her leg and sent her immediately over to the emergency room. Gangrene had set into the wound, and it had to be lanced and thoroughly cleaned out. She was rushed into surgery in an attempt to save her leg. After three days in the hospital and an array of antibiotics, she was sent home with about one-third of her shin missing. They saved the leg, but she lost a good deal of circulation to her foot and faced a significant recovery time.

The hardest part of all of this was that I never knew anything about this incident until months later. I was never told about the injury, the infection, the hospitalization, or the surgery until two to three months later. I was home for a visit in the spring, and Mom showed me her scar and made light of the story. When asked why no one told me, I received the pat answer, "We didn't want you to worry."

Mom's cover-up was about keeping me from knowing that she was continuing to make poor decisions about her capabilities as an eighty-two-year-old.

When I was home the next time, I went to grab a coffee cup for my morning caffeine fix when I noticed the coffee mug had old dried coffee in the bottom. The kitchen floor was so dirty that my feet were sticking to it. When setting the table for dinner, I noticed the dishes in the cabinet were still dirty. The kitchen was always Mom's pride and joy, so to see things in such a state gave me great cause for concern.

The following winter was an unusually harsh one (even for Buffalo, New York). We were living in Tennessee at the time, and I knew from the weather information that Buffalo was in the midst of below-zero temperatures and over thirty inches of snow. I called home to check on my parents, and of course, no one answered the phone (this was frequently the case as they would hang the phone up without placing it completely on the base). I called several other times over the twenty-four hours and finally gave up and called a neighbor's cell phone. The neighbor advised that the power had been out for the last two days. She was kind enough to check on them for me and advised they had been sitting in the dark for the last forty-eight-plus hours without any heat. The neighbor found them bundled up in blankets, sitting in the living room recliners. A candle provided their only light, and they had been eating a steady diet of peanut butter and jelly sandwiches.

Once again, this left me feeling guilty about being so far away and unable to be there to help them. The guilt was heartbreaking.

4

On the Road

No. 4 "Haven't Seen It Yet" by Danny Gokey

At eighty-four and eighty-six years of age, Mom and Dad are still driving. On my last visit, I found myself riding down the middle of the street at about 15 mph, begging my dad to let me drive! *(it was frightening, honestly)*.

The real treat was when I found myself in the back seat of my parents' car as Mom relentlessly corrected Dad's driving skills, and he got more aggravated by the moment. At *forty-something*, I am right back in my teens as my parents assume the driving role.

Dad had never really liked Mom to drive, and he was determined not to relinquish his authority now. Their trips were always short to and from the grocery store or to church. They may not have been long, but they were clearly frightening.

I knew it was time to get them off the road, but how could I ever hope to be successful when I was still being treated like a child, relegated to the back seat? During this particular visit, Dad attempted to pull the car into the single-door garage. He managed to take the side view mirror off and scrape the entire right side of the vehicle on the door casing.

When I got out to inspect the damage, I looked at the back wall in the garage and noticed that the 1930s steel filing cabinet had a huge dent in one of the drawers. Dad proceeded to share that Mom had mistakenly put the car in drive when backing out of the garage a few weeks earlier and smashed into the file cabinet.

Mom was so critical of Dad's driving that she would often head out on her own. She was actually a slightly better driver than Dad, but she was consistent about taking two parking places and felt like many stop signs were optional.

I knew I needed to get the keys, but it was not going to be easy. I began my quest by checking their licenses and found that Mom's license had expired almost a year. Dad's license was still valid until the following May, but I knew his recent vision loss was affecting his peripheral and depth perception.

I surfaced the issue of Mom's expired license, and Dad recognized the risk immediately. He tried to assume all the driving, but Mom would not accept the facts. The arguing went on for hours, and I actually left that evening to return home. Dad drove me to the airport in silence, and I left feeling like I was the enemy that came to town to disrupt my parents' lives. I remember sobbing as I waited for my plane to board.

About two weeks later, I received a call from the Amherst Police Department advising that Dad had been in a severe car accident. Dad proceeded to turn left after the turn arrow had ended, and a pickup truck hit him broadside. He was pinned in the car, and EMS had to use the jaws of life to get him out of the vehicle. The car was totaled. Dad was taken to the hospital with a concussion and a broken collarbone.

I hopped on the next flight and went directly to the hospital from the airport. Dad was in a lot of pain from a fractured collarbone and bruised pelvis but had no recollection of the accident. He was discharged the next day with a myriad of pain medications.

As if the accident wasn't enough chaos, Mom's behavior after this trauma was shocking. She showed no concern for Dad or his health. She was overwhelmingly focused on the costs and inconveniences tied to the loss of the vehicle. She was obsessed with worrying over what was going to happen to their insurance and what she was going to do without a car. This disconnected emotional reaction was disturbing, to say the least. I later learned that dementia could cause this type of twisted response. When the brain is damaged, it will often rewire itself to create new, unexpected connections. This rewiring will also present as irrational emotional behavior.

I took a week off work to help Dad recover and was continually shocked at Mom's hateful comments about Dad. She blamed him for the accident. She didn't care about filling his prescriptions, and when he was clearly in pain, she showed no compassion.

I felt like a referee the entire visit. I took on the responsibility of getting the insurance claim filed. I had to explain the insurance claim process over and over again and lost the battle regarding the need for a rental car. The notion of getting transportation from the senior center or church was deemed ridiculous. It was time for me to get back to my family and work, so I left town reluctantly with a rental car in their driveway.

5

The First Few Swings

Now it is abundantly clear that it's time to get some help. I reached out to cousins who had been through a similar situation with their mother, called the Alzheimer's Association, spoke with my own family doctor, and although everyone wanted to help, there was really nothing further they could do—especially long distance.

The next few weeks were filled with what I call "The Tough Conversations." My most immediate need was to get my mom off the road while Dad was recovering. I needed both parents to understand that Mom could no longer legally drive. Her license had expired months ago, and she was in no mental capacity to continue driving. I showed Mom the expired license multiple times, and of course, it didn't register as a fact. Dad understood that the license had expired but was too weak to fight with Mom about it. He simply avoided the argument by saying he would handle the situation once he felt better.

The next swing was about getting help with the general house upkeep. My suggestion that they consider hiring a housekeeper and perhaps a neighborhood teen to mow the lawn was simply preposterous and deemed insulting. I even offered to pay for it. That was more insulting!

My husband, Bill, became my "uncertified therapist" and listened for endless hours as I struggled through this difficult time. He wiped my tears away and constantly stood beside me every time I took a "swing" at trying to help my parents, and they shot me down.

I called the church my dad had attended for as long as I can remember and asked for some help from their senior minister. Turns out they didn't have one, but they had a team of individuals that performed "senior outreach" services. A wonderful couple from the church called me and agreed to make a visit to Mom and Dad's home. They arrived at the house; Dad met them at the door but would not let them in. "Thank you for stopping by, we are doing just fine," was the extent of their visit. The family sent the pastor to visit a few days later, and he got the same greeting.

I worried about what they were eating, so I arranged for Meals on Wheels to begin bringing meals to them. The first visit was reluctantly accepted by my dad, but I later learned that Mom threw the food out. They came by the next day, and Mom told them to keep their food.

I found a local housekeeper that I hired to try to come in once a month to do a thorough cleaning, and that never got off the ground because Mom would not let them in the house. Both of my parents were simply furious with me at this point in the journey. Mom would not come to the phone when I called, and Dad was quite short with me as well. I knew it was time for another visit. I told them I was coming home, and for the first time, I was told "not to bother." Dad explained that Mom was still quite upset that I would ask strangers to come into our home and clean, and she was very offended when I tried to make nutritious meals available through Meals on Wheels. Dad also said he was embarrassed that the church people came out to visit them. I was told it might be best to focus on my own family and leave things alone in Buffalo. Needless to say, I was crushed.

I let a few weeks go by, but by now, fall was approaching, and I began to worry about the upcoming winter. If you've never been to Buffalo, they measure snow by the foot versus by the inch in Western New York.

I decided I needed to take another swing and hopped on another flight back home, this time unannounced. I walked up the driveway, and both Mom and Dad were sitting in their favorite lawn chairs on the front porch. They were both visibly shocked to see me. The very first question was, how long will you be here? It stung not to be welcomed.

Dad was the one to try to cover for Mom's harshness as her dementia progressed. He would make excuses for her behavior and apologize as best he could. This trip was one of the most difficult to date.

We had our usual catch-up conversation, and I offered to take them out to dinner. Mom immediately declined, but Dad insisted she go. After another heated argument, we got in the car and headed for one of their favorite local restaurants for the famous "beef on wick" roast beef sandwich.

I noticed Mom was very uncomfortable in the restaurant. Our conversation was strained at best. Many times, she would not even look at me. Finally, that night, all the pent-up anger came rushing out in my direction.

We were sitting in the living room when I brought up the topic of securing a power of attorney to handle their affairs in the event that they were unable to do so. You would have thought I dropped a bomb on the coffee table. Mom released a tsunami of hurtful accusations:

"What's wrong with you? You are so determined to take over our house, our money, take our car away, tell people to watch out for us... Why don't you just mind your own business? We have told you hundreds of times that we don't need your help. The things you have been doing over the last six months are embarrassing to us. We've never asked anyone to help us, and we sure as *hell* won't start now. We really wish you would just leave us alone."

Dad stepped in as the mediator at that moment and tried to soften the blow by turning the discussion to the fact that they had already drawn up their will, and he didn't see the need for a POA. I explained that the POA allows someone to act on their behalf while they are still living. A will is simply direction on how to allocate resources upon death. He agreed to simply look into it, which was basically his way of getting me off the subject.

Tempers flared, and between my tears, I rattled off the list of things that I had observed or experienced that had caused my concern. Car accidents, expired licenses, out-of-date foods in the refrigerator and pantry, housekeeping issues, Mom's fall and hospitalization, lawn care, and Dad's health. Needless to say, that was a mistake. Mom walked out of the room and began the famous silent treatment. Dad agreed that I was too harsh and had no business judging them. I retreated to the guest room.

About thirty minutes later, I wandered out of the room to use the restroom when I overheard my parents talking about me in a less than favorable vain. I overheard things like, "I wish she would just get the hell out of our house. All she's after is our money. She's got her own family now, why is she meddling in our lives?"

Dad would try to calm Mom down by assuring her that he would speak with me in the morning, but she started breaking glasses and plates on the floor. I came out to see what the commotion was, and Mom told me to get out. She was screaming so loud that her face was bright red, and the veins in her neck were bulging. I had never seen her behave this way. I was frightened and returned to the guest room. I filled the rest of the evening with more tears. Once again, my husband got the tearful phone call recapping the latest set of arguments.

I couldn't sleep that night, so I decided to put my feelings down on paper for Dad to read. I wrote a letter outlining the fact that my reasons for trying to help were all rooted in my love for them. I wanted some evidence (somewhere) that I was not the evil child trying to destroy their lives. I outlined a list of three things that I wanted him to consider: identify a power of attorney, get Mom off the road, and consider getting some help for things around the house.

The next morning was all about the silent treatment. No one said anything. I went out to the grocery store to reload the refrigerator. When I came home, Mom was outside, so I proceeded to weed out the spoiled food and replace it with the new items (I took great care to buy the same brands and the same sizes that she always bought so she would not know that I had made the swap). I also had to take all the spoiled food directly to the outside trash can so I could avoid another argument.

That afternoon, I left my letter on the table and took a cab to the airport. Once again, I had failed at the latest attempt to try to help my aging parents.

6

Being the Punching Bag

No. 5 "You Raise Me Up" by Josh Groban

I let a few days go by before resuming my check-in calls. There was no answer, and of course, the answering machine I had set up for them was not turned on. The phone just rang and rang. I knew they didn't have caller ID, but I was convinced they were somehow screening my calls. As time went on, I grew increasingly concerned.

After two days of failed phone calling, I reached out to the next-door neighbor who had been kind enough to keep an eye on Mom and Dad for me. She went over to the house and reported back that the ringer had been turned off on the phone. When she told them I had been trying to reach them, my mom quickly replied, "I wish she would just leave us alone."

Relieved that they were okay, I was still so hurt by their words and actions. The sting resonated for weeks. I was worried all the time. I felt like whatever I did was wrong. If I did nothing, I was wrong. If I tried to offer or provide solutions, I was wrong. All I wanted to do was keep them safe, and somehow, I turned into the enemy. It was truly a heartbreaking time.

I would lay awake worrying about Dad's health, driving, safety, and hundreds of other things that could go wrong. I felt guilty because I didn't live close enough to be there for them. I was beating myself up whenever my parents weren't doing it for me.

The calls home became more strained. The conversation didn't come easy. Calls got shorter. Nothing was ever new with them. Dad would make small talk, but Mom would seldom come to the phone.

That Christmas, my husband and I extended an invitation to come to visit us. The flights were booked online, and all they had to do was arrange to get to and from the airport. Our children were still quite young at the time, and Dad was excited about being together for the holidays. Mom, on the other hand, was quite reluctant. After much argument, they agreed to fly for the first time in forty years. They had gotten lost in the airport and almost missed their connection, but somehow made it safely.

From the moment they arrived in Mobile, Alabama, it was one argument after another. Mom was so critical of Dad's every move. *"He walks too slow," "He can't see," "He can't hear," "He coughs all the time," "He's so miserable," "He's lazy,"* and on and on. What we didn't know at the time was just how sick he really was. He never told anyone, but he was suffering from kidney cancer and had an aortic aneurysm that could rupture at any time. He had lost vision in his left eye as a result of a vascular issue in his optic nerve. The man was truly ill, and she was unmerciful in her criticism of him. He was her punching bag.

Dad was not known for his unending patience. He would lose his temper often, and the arguing would go on for hours. That Christmas, the kids noticed Grandma kept repeating the same stories. She kept forgetting their names and often called me by my cousin's name. She would quickly recover, but it was definitely more obvious.

One morning, during their visit, we heard a huge thud from their bedroom. Mom had gotten out of bed, lost her balance, and hit her head on the nightstand. She had a significant cut on her head and ended up with two black eyes.

During that same visit, Dad complained of severe back pain, and we ended up taking him to the hospital. All his medical treatment was through the Veterans Administration, so we had to take him to Biloxi, Mississippi, which was the closest VA hospital. This hour trip ended with his getting admitted. He spent the next seven days in the hospital. We drove back and forth to visit with him every day. His diagnosis was kept from all of us at the time, but it was actually his kidney cancer that caused his pain.

Whenever Mom would speak of Dad, she would say the most hurtful things. She showed no compassion for him and kept insisting that they never should have tried to make the trip. Our kids would get on Mom's nerves. She insisted on helping in the kitchen and with the laundry. It was well intended, but dishes were put away dirty, and socks were mismatched. I was repeatedly reminded of what an awful job I was doing at keeping a tidy home.

Once Dad was released, they hopped on the next flight back to Buffalo with two black eyes and a bag full of prescription medication for Dad. It was a stressful holiday for all.

Our household took many weeks to recover.

7

❦

Now I'm Scared

No. 6 "I Know" by Big Daddy Weave

I know Dad's health is declining. It was clear Mom's cognitive state was deteriorating. Their pride and stubborn nature were not allowing them to face the obvious. Now I realize it will be up to me to see them through this final part of their journey. I'm confused, scared, and completely unprepared.

Buffalo got hit with one of its usual monstrous snow storms that year, and I knew Dad could not clear the driveway by himself. I hired a plow service to clear their driveway and never told them. When we spoke on the phone, I told them a neighbor must have cleared it for them.

I asked the neighbors to stop in and check on my parents. We developed a plan where a different neighbor stopped by every two days. The neighbors took it upon themselves to bring a covered dish or some baked goods whenever they stopped in. The neighbors would give me a call after each visit to provide an update. During one of the visits, the neighbor mentioned Dad had bought a new car. Evidently, it was a big sedan that barely fit in the one-car garage.

When I asked about the car, it was confirmed, and Mom went on about how the car was too big and Dad was a fool to have pur-

20

chased it. Two weeks later, they traded the sedan in for a Toyota Corolla. Keep in mind that these cars were sold to them without valid driver's licenses. I was furious.

Next, I got a call from a neighbor that informed me that Mom had been in an accident. Turns out she went to the bank to do their weekly set of transactions. When she was leaving the parking lot, she thought she had the car in reverse when it was actually in drive. She went up over the curb and smashed into the huge window on the side of the bank. The glass shattered, but thankfully it was like windshield glass and did not fall on the car. The police got involved and cited her for driving with an invalid license. Of course, this event was left out of the conversations in my many calls home.

Now I'm frightened for them and for others they might put at risk. It was time for another flight home.

Everybody's Angry

Dad now realizes the risks associated with Mom's continued driving. He's angry. Mom's furious because someone is trying to tell her what to do. I'm angry because I have to burn another three to four days of vacation and the cost of another flight to come home. Things are coming to a head.

I no longer asked my parents to pick me up at the airport, so I hopped in my rental car and prayed that this visit might be a positive and productive one.

As I approached the house, I noticed the gutters were coming off the house. Fall was coming, and it would definitely be a problem as winter approached.

When I walked into the house, Dad was sitting at the kitchen table reading the paper with his magnifying glass. He had recently suffered some kind of mini-stroke that resulted in the loss of vision in his right eye. Mom was in her favorite recliner in the living room. Dad stood up to greet me, and Mom did not say a word. He had to call her to tell her I had arrived. She pretended to be glad to welcome me home, but it was clearly not her best effort.

As I glanced around the kitchen, it was clear that the floors needed to be mopped. I reached for a glass in the cupboard, and it had something still in the bottom. I found a clean one and reached into the refrigerator for a cold sweet tea. The milk was out of date, and I found an opened can of tuna with plastic wrap stretched across the top (that's something she would have never done in the past). I ignored it for the moment and sat at the kitchen table with Dad.

His first words to me were, "Let's make this a nice visit this time. Don't upset your mother. We all know she has been forgetting things lately, but don't bring that up this trip. Okay?" I told him that I could not ignore things any longer and that it was time to begin developing a plan to address the fact that it's no longer safe for both of you to be at home without help. He agreed it had been a little rough lately, but they will work things out. "I really shouldn't get involved." Once again, I ran headfirst into another brick wall.

I went in to visit Mom, and she immediately started in with complaints about Dad. She made sure I went out to the garage to inspect the newest damage caused by "the car he never should have purchased because it was too big for the garage." (Dad had hit both sides of the garage door with the side mirror of the new car.) "He's so miserable," "He's completely useless," and on and on. The more she had to say, the angrier I got. Dad overheard her comments, and the fights resumed.

Dad was weakened by the kidney cancer he refused to treat. It hurt my heart to see Mom so critical of a man that was truly ill. She was more concerned about how much work he needed to get done that he was unable to do and the costs associated with his recent hospital trips than she was about his health.

Later that evening, I slipped into the kitchen and began throwing out all the spoiled or questionable foods. I was wiping out the refrigerator when Mom walked in and asked me what I was doing.

I told her that I had to throw several expired items out, and she got furious. She felt like that was wasteful. I grabbed the keys and went out to the grocery store to replenish the fridge. When I came in with the groceries, she insisted it was unnecessary but was also excited about some of the unexpected goodies I picked up along the way. We baked cookies that evening and enjoyed a little television together.

I decided that the next morning would be my moment to address the need for change. That was absolutely the hardest conversation I have ever had. I remember it like it was yesterday.

I started by expressing my concern. They dismissed any reason for me to be concerned. I moved to my frustration over the things I tried to put in place for them that they had refused. Those things were also unnecessary and ridiculous. I progressed into my anger surrounding the fact that I am continually worried and fearful for them. I also addressed the fact that I cannot continue to take time away from my young family and career to wrangle over potential solutions. They got angry too and told me to leave. "We don't need your help. Leave us alone."

I left the house that afternoon in tears. I wasn't sure where I was going to go, but I knew I had to leave their home. I found myself parked in a mall parking lot about three miles away and just sat there and sobbed for what seemed like hours. I called my husband, recounted the most recent argument, and he simply said, "Enough is Enough. Just come home."

I called the airline and rebooked my flight home for later that evening. Once I got myself together, I went back to the house to pack my things. Tensions were high, and they both knew they had deeply hurt my feelings. Dad pulled me aside to apologize for Mom's behavior and admitted for the first time that she was "not herself." I didn't say much; I threw my bag in the car and headed for the airport.

9

Taking Its Toll

No. 7 "Word of God Speak" by Mercy Me

When I got home, I decided to reach out to anyone that might be able to help me with this situation. I spoke with the Alzheimer's Association and began attending a local support group. I reached out to my cousin, who went through a very similar situation with her mom. I even attended a seminar put on at a local assisted living facility. Although each of these actions were helpful in some way, none of them could help me eliminate the constant worry and the overpowering guilt I felt. I found myself having difficulty sleeping (which has always been one of my favorite things to do). My responsibilities at work were relentless, and the pressure was beginning to take its toll on me.

One evening, I woke up from a sound sleep. My heart was racing, and I was short of breath. I was soaking wet from sweat, and I was completely petrified. I woke Bill up and asked him to take me to the emergency room. I thought I was having a heart attack. In a matter of minutes, we were flying down the road toward the nearest hospital. I can't really recall much of what happened that night, but there was no waiting in the emergency room. They put me on a gurney in the lobby and rushed me back to begin monitoring my heart.

I'm told the beats per minute were well over one hundred. Turns out this was the first (of what would turn out to be many) anxiety attacks.

I was admitted for observation and ended up staying in that hospital for three days. My diagnosis was acute anxiety and extreme fatigue. The doctors insisted I pass a stress test before I could be discharged. I was prescribed a regular regimen of medication and told to eliminate as much stress as possible. I simply smiled, thanked the physician for getting me through this episode, and agreed to do my best.

I was given a hard dose of reality regarding the effects of stress on our health. I didn't even realize what was happening until my body just reacted in the most frightening way. My prayer is that you might learn from my story and never allow the stress of your dementia journey to impact your health.

10

The Fall

No. 8 "Famous For" by Tauren Wells

It had been almost four months since I had spoken to my parents. I stopped the weekly phone calls and made no plans to visit. It was a September evening when I got the dreaded call from my parents next door neighbor. "Thought you should know that EMS is at your parent's house, and they are taking your mom to the hospital." My heart sank and started racing. She didn't have much detail at the time but wanted me to be aware of the situation.

She was able to find out what hospital they were taking my mom to, so I tracked down the nurse that was caring for her in the emergency room. She advised that mom was stable and told me that the physician treating her would call as soon as he finished his assessment.

I called Dad, and he was completely overwhelmed. He kept saying, "I thought she needed to go to the hospital, but she kept refusing to do so." I didn't quite understand what he meant by that statement until days later.

As it turns out, Mom was up on the ladder three days prior, cleaning out the leaves from the gutters of the house. She lost her balance and fell to the ground. She was in a great deal of pain but managed to hobble into the house and get to the bedroom. Dad did not see her fall and had no idea why she was in such pain. She called for aspirin (as that was the only medication she would ever take), and Dad gave it to her as requested.

She didn't get up from bed for over twelve hours and finally tried to make her way to the bathroom. She fell on the floor next to bed in excruciating pain. She had to empty her bladder, and Dad simply sopped it up with towels. She refused his offer to help her back to the bed. He was frozen in fear. He knew what was logical and appropriate yet delayed calling an ambulance for two more days. His ability to reasonably act in this situation was a clear indication that his dementia was progressing rapidly. I later learned that Mom threatened to kill him if he called for help. She was convinced that she would heal on her own.

By day three, Mom was severely dehydrated, and rigor had begun to set into her joints as she lay on the floor. She was now delirious from both pain and lack of nourishment. Dad finally called 911.

When the emergency room physician called me back, he advised that Mom had fractured her hip. She was severely dehydrated, so they would have to give her fluids and schedule the surgery in the morning. I advised I would be on the next plane to Buffalo to be there when she came out of surgery.

That's exactly what I did. I was in the recovery room when she woke up, and she was still not happy to see me. Even in the aftermath of major surgery, her first words were, "When can I get out of here?"

The doctors advised that she would have a couple of days in recovery and then be discharged to a rehab facility for up to one hundred days. Immediately, I knew that I had to get busy looking for solutions for both her and Dad. He could no longer stay at home on his own.

The hospital gave me their recommendation on rehabilitation facilities in the area, so I set out to begin the enrollment process for Mom and find an assisted living facility for Dad. As it turned out, he could stay on the same property while Mom was recovering. I thought that was an amazing solution as they promised to get him over to see her on a daily basis.

After filling out hundreds of papers and locating insurance cards, Medicare details, social security numbers, and writing multiple checks, they were successfully enrolled. I stayed with Dad for two days until Mom was released from the hospital. We packed his things and got him settled in what we called his "temporary apartment." We met the transport when Mom arrived at the rehab facility and visited her room for a while.

She was not happy about the fact that she still had to stay in "this awful place," but we all knew she did not have a choice. We explained that Dad was going to be in a nearby apartment where he would be well-fed and taken care of while she was recovering. I also assured her that Dad would be coming by regularly to see her. That was somewhat good news to her, but her biggest concern was who was going to pay for all of this. She felt it was unnecessary and a colossal waste of money.

It was time for me to get back to my own family and back to work. Once again, I head back to the airport, exhausted and worried.

11

The Storm

Once settled back at home, I began the daily calls to Dad and to the rehabilitation facility to get regular updates. Dad had a phone in his room but often left it off the hook, so I would have to contact the community to go down to his room to get connected with him. The therapists in rehab assured me that Mom was making appropriate progress. She was only two days into therapy when she was already beginning to bear weight on the once-fractured hip.

When I would chat with Dad, he would tell me that all was well with him. He wanted to go over to visit Mom, but the staff had yet to take him over to the rehabilitation section of the community. When I asked about it, they told me they would absolutely follow up, and the next day, I would have an identical conversation with both Dad and the assisted living community.

I finally tracked down a member of the management staff and was told that Dad was refusing to let them help him with showers and was not coming out of the room for meals. They assured me they would take him over that afternoon for a visit with Mom.

Concerned about the fact that Dad was not eating (as well as bathing), I asked my beloved neighbor to stop in for a visit. She reported back to me that he said no one was coming to get him for meals, and no one had been in to see him at all in the eight or so days since I had left town. She mentioned that he needed a shower and a shave as well.

Now I'm furious. The facility was not cheap, and collectively, they were charging over $11,000 per month for both of my parents to reside with them. I made another phone call to the management and was assured it would all be addressed immediately. Later that evening, I called Dad to find out that he did get to visit Mom. She was still in a good deal of pain but appeared to be doing quite well. When I asked him if he had eaten, he couldn't remember. He assured me he was doing fine and didn't want me to worry.

Being free from worry was not something I was experiencing at the time. In fact, I was more overwhelmed with worry than ever before. After much prayer, I realized that embedded in this horrible set of circumstances was likely the blessing I needed to finally get my parents the care they desperately needed.

I knew Mom was never going to be able to be safe in her home again. Dad was clearly not able to take care of her. I knew this was my best opportunity to convince them to move to a senior living community. I spoke with Dad about it, and he made it clear he wanted to stay in Buffalo.

The fact that he recognized that both of them would actually benefit from some assistance was a major breakthrough. I took full advantage of his willingness to look for suitable care facilities and headed back to Buffalo the following week.

Mom's recovery continued to progress very well, and when I arrived three weeks later, she was walking with a walker. I greeted her in the rehabilitation community, and no sooner had I finished hugging her when she asked, "When can I get out of here and go back to my home?" This was a significant blow to my hopeful plans for that visit.

Next, I went to visit Dad on the assisted living side of the community. I walked into his room, and it literally stunk. He needed a shave, the room was a mess, and he was very thin. His linens needed to be changed, and he clearly needed a shower. I asked him what the facility was doing for him, and he said nothing. He hadn't seen anyone in a few days, and he was very anxious about getting the newspaper delivered to his room (the paper he was reading was the previous Sunday edition, six days old). The TV in his room was not working, and I just felt awful for leaving him in such a situation. I found the manager on duty and brought them to the room to observe what I had found. She was shocked, very apologetic, and was going to look into things for me and the excuses went on and on. I was furious and felt like I failed him when he needed my help the most. It was awful.

This experience was not helping my case for finding an assisted living community for my parents. Dad's perspective is now tainted, and he had seen no value whatsoever in living in a community setting. "I can do this better myself. At least at home, I know where things are, and I can make myself a sandwich or something when I need it," were his words, and honestly, I couldn't argue his point.

I was successful in getting him to visit two other communities that weekend. He went in, looked around the common area, and walked through one room in each community. He found them to be much too small and was immediately concerned about the cost. I tried to convince him that his insurance would cover all the costs, but he insisted on taking all the community sales collateral and agreed to review it.

He was completely exhausted after viewing these communities, so we went out for a cold beer and a sandwich at his favorite local pub. Buffalo is famous for its chicken wings and fish fry meals. This Irish pub had both those options for him to enjoy. He ate the biggest meal I have seen him eat in many months. After dinner, he wanted to go back to their home. He said he needed to pick up a few things, but he really wanted to stay there for the night. I was going to be there anyway, so we agreed to spend the night together and go visit Mom in the morning.

12

The Tsunami

No. 9 "Hold Me Jesus" by Big Daddy Weave

When I wandered into the kitchen the next morning, Dad had his magnifying glass out and was pouring over the details in the senior community's sales brochures. He would take meticulous notes to help him remember all the details. Next, he would develop a laundry list of questions to help him remember what he wanted to ask of either me or the community representative.

Before I could finish my first cup of coffee, the notes and questions were already multiple pages. I tried to ask if there were any questions I might answer and was abruptly told, "Just let me finish this."

A *tsunami* is defined as an unusually large sea wave caused by a volcanic eruption. Storm experts know that they can occur, but they erupt unexpectedly with powerfully damaging results. Well, the events of the next few days felt like a tsunami to me.

Dad finished his analysis on the assisted living option we explored together and couldn't get past the pricing. When he found out that their costs would be well over $6,000, he blew a gasket, as I say. "Why would you ever think that your mother and I would ever spend that kind of money when we have a wonderful home that is fully paid for? Why do you continue to insist that we need help? Once Mom gets home, we'll be just fine on our own."

I gently reminded him that Mom had fallen and laid on the floor for three days before help was requested. He told me that was only because she wouldn't let him call EMS. "It was a very unusual circumstance, and it would never happen again." I also reminded him of his physical weakness. I told him the veteran's administration doctor shared his cancer diagnosis with me and explained that his weakness and fatigue were likely to increase in the months to come. This statement caused a volcanic eruption. Dad had forgotten that he had listed me as his healthcare power of attorney and was furious that I knew his diagnosis.

"None of this is any of your business. You continually force your nose into places it does not belong, and it has to stop!" he screamed.

In the midst of this argument, I got a call from Mom's rehab facility. They reported that her behavior was uncooperative and that they were unable to complete her therapy that particular day. She was argumentative and threw her walker across the room. She also told the therapist to *"get out!"* and *"leave me alone."* She was requesting to speak to both myself and Dad.

We hopped in the car and traveled the fifteen minutes to the facility in silence. When we arrived, the therapy team met us at the entrance and escorted us to her room. She was furious. Screaming at the top of her lungs about how these people were holding her prisoner and that she needed us to get her out of there immediately. Dad tried to calm her down, and she told him it was his fault she was in this awful place. Next, she turned to me and told me that I needed to get her home. She somehow felt like I might be her ally in this situation.

I had to tell her the painful truth. She needed to stay for her own health and safety. That was *not* what she wanted to hear, and her ranting kept getting louder and louder.

I left the room and asked the therapist to explain to Mom why she needed this rehabilitation. The therapist started to explain the recovery process for a fractured hip, and before she could finish the first sentence, my mom cut her off, "You people don't know what you are doing. I can heal just as well at home. This is just a money-making ploy. I don't need your help." They finally came in with a sedative for her as she was completely out of control. This was both scary and embarrassing.

We stayed until she fell asleep, and both Dad and I felt like we had just been hit by a truck. He was visibly upset, and my nerves were completely shot.

On the way home, I checked my work voicemail and discovered there was an issue with a key customer that I was responsible for. The client was livid, and my team had been trying to reach me to assist with a solution. I had made an error that impacted the customer's consumer communication, more stress.

After an hour or so of damage control, the work situation was under control, but the team was clearly frustrated with the amount of time I had been away from my role. My boss dropped several hints at how concerned he was becoming over my time off the job.

Dad and I stayed at their home again that night and discussed the day's events over a bowl of ice cream after dinner. He insisted that Mom was just not herself. "She's a tough old coot, and she doesn't like people to tell her what to do, you know!" was his assessment. I was exhausted and unable to begin another argument, so I simply went to bed.

To top off an already miserable day, I called home to find out that my husband was stressed over trying to manage his career and carry a full load of caring for the children. He was also getting impacted by this ongoing turn of events. I, of course, felt guilty and helpless in this situation as well.

As difficult as today had been, I went to bed that night, praying for the wisdom to find my way through this situation. As I reflect, I realize how many people are being affected by the fact that two individuals have allowed their health and dementia to decline to a state that now prevents them from making sound, rational decisions. I don't blame Mom and Dad, but I just wish they would allow me to help them.

13

No More Choices

No. 10 "God Speaking" by Mandisa

After sixty days of rehab, Mom's doctors say she cannot go back to her home.

Dad has lost another twenty pounds he couldn't afford to lose. His cough is becoming more uncontrollable, and he is sleeping the better part of every day.

My absence at work is beginning to affect the rest of my work team, and my absence at home was wearing on both my husband and the children.

We are officially out of options. Making some tough decisions was no longer something that could be postponed.

I walked into the kitchen that morning to find Dad with his cup of coffee pouring over the newspaper. I had made the decision that I needed to be as straightforward and direct as possible, so I simply said, "Dad, I can't do this anymore."

"I can't continue to try to reason with you and Mom any longer. I can't continue to worry about your health and safety. I can't hop on a plane and leave my work and family every other week. We know that Mom cannot return to this home safely. You can't take care of her yourself. You won't let anyone come in to help. You won't try any other living options that will provide what you need. I'm tired. I'm done."

After I completed my rant, Dad simply stared down at the newspaper, head down for what seemed like an eternity. The quiet was deafening.

Finally, he said, "You're right. Your mother needs more help than I can provide. She's not going to like it, but we have no choice but to figure out what we are going to do about it."

I had prayed for those words for literally *years*, yet when they finally came, they were laden with sadness. It was like Dad had been defeated. The look on his face at that moment is embedded in my heart. He was clearly brokenhearted, and I felt totally responsible.

I told him I was glad that he had finally reached this conclusion. I tried to assure him that things would all work out, but he just looked at me and walked into the other room.

We spent the next few hours in silence, and I began the process of exploring assisted living options. It was clear we would not consider the facility that they were currently staying in, so my "Google search" began.

By now, Mom had completed about two-thirds of her one hundred days of rehabilitation. That left us with about forty days to devise and execute what was bound to be a very complex plan.

That evening, I told Dad that I had three places lined up for us to visit the following day. He remembered our last set of community tours (before mom's fall) and refused to go back to any of those facilities. That eliminated two of the communities right off the bat. He went on to say, "If we found a suitable place, it was only going to be until Mom could get better—nothing permanent."

That sent me back to what felt like "square one," but I decided to take whatever cooperation I could get and keep moving forward.

The next morning, we set out to visit four new communities in the Buffalo area. In each tour, Dad interrupted the salesperson with questions on pricing. As you can imagine, there was something wrong with each and every one of the communities. Too small, felt like a hospital, Mom wouldn't like any of them, and of course, they were all too expensive.

After that colossal waste of everyone's time, Dad was exhausted. We went back to the house, and he took another extensive nap. During that time, I crafted the idea of telling him that I discovered that they were eligible for some insurance assistance to hopefully alleviate some of his pricing concerns. It was a fib, of course, but only a partial one, as I had recently learned that they were likely eligible for a veteran's assistance program.

That evening, I shared my insurance fib and the details surrounding the veteran's aid and assistance program (just FYI, there is no coverage in Medicare for assisted living, but the VA program could potentially cover $2,100 per month). I told Dad I would work to get the entire cost of their new apartment covered via these two avenues. He seemed encouraged.

I also thought I would seed the idea of selecting a location that was in the Charlotte area, so we could all be together, and I could eliminate the travel back and forth to Buffalo. Surprisingly, he liked the idea of shifting the search to Charlotte. He added, "That might work, seeing as it was only temporary." Again, my heart sank.

The following morning, we went to visit Mom together. We decided in advance not to tell her of our upcoming moving plans. I walked Dad back to his apartment, and I headed back to Charlotte with the task of finding a suitable senior living solution that would be available within the next few weeks.

14

Shopping for Assisted Living

We had not been living in the Charlotte area for very long, so in addition to learning all about the senior living industry, I had the added challenge of navigating a new city.

Work grew increasingly more stressful, our children were in college now (so finances were tight), and the challenges continued to manifest back in Buffalo.

Mom was improving in rehab, but her dementia behaviors were making it nearly impossible for the therapists to work with her. I had to have three conference calls with the therapy team to convince them not to discharge her. Dad's health took a turn for the worse, and he ended up in the hospital for dehydration and bronchial pneumonia.

My search for senior living required me to learn an entirely different language, so it seemed. I discovered there are numerous hidden costs that you need to be aware of. I learned about the level of care fees, medication management fees, and community fees, to mention a few. I learned to pay close attention to the staff versus the physical appearance of the facility. I had to learn about care plans, activities of daily living, DNR, POAs, Medicare, and the list goes on and on.

Finally, after three weeks and fifteen-plus tours, I settled on a suitable solution for Mom and Dad. Next began the preparation work for their admission (physical exams, tuberculosis tests, medication orders, packing, securing furniture, bedding, and of course, booking flights to get to Buffalo and back with Mom and Dad).

15

The Move

No. 11 "You Are Loved" by Josh Groban

One hundred days of rehabilitation had come to an end, and all the plans were in place to move to Charlotte.

Bill and I flew into Buffalo, rented a car, and stayed at Mom and Dad's home that evening. The next morning, we arrived at the community in Buffalo to find that the staff already had Mom dressed, packed, and waiting in the lobby (*I tried not to read into that too much!*). Mom was all excited to be going back to her "little house," as she called it.

Dad was operating under the notion that this would be a temporary trip to Charlotte, and Bill wasn't sure what to say to either party, so he just tried to stay positive and nod a lot.

I waited until we got everyone loaded in the car to tell Mom that the doctors had changed some plans regarding her recuperation. I broke the news that she was going to spend some time closer to us and her grandchildren for the next few weeks.

Her reply was, as expected, "I certainly am not."

Dad tried to intervene to assure her it was all temporary and that she didn't have a choice. She didn't like that answer and tried to open the car door.

"I'll walk home if I have to."

We tried to change the subject as we headed to the airport and stopped for a cup of coffee and some of Mom's favorite donuts. She loved the idea for a moment and seemed to forget the recently communicated change of plans.

She enjoyed her donut and coffee, and mid-donut, she wanted to know where we are going. We pulled up to the unloading area at the airport unloaded her wheelchair, and she refused to get out of the car. She grew increasingly upset and actually threw up all over my husband. Now everyone was upset; the airport police were flagging us to move along, Mom's screaming, and Dad had to yell at her to get her to finally transfer to the wheelchair.

Bill got cleaned up, returned the rental car, and met us at the gate. Security was another battle, but I think you get the picture.

As we sat at the gate, the behavior continued. She accused all of us of lying to her. I tried to focus on the fact that she was going to be with Dad and close enough for all of my family to visit regularly, but that was of no concern. After about an hour or so rant, she was worn out and sat quietly with a huge scowl on her face while we waited to board.

When we got our boarding passes, we discovered that we were seated in the very rear of the aircraft. Our seats had been changed for some unknown reason, and Mom had to slowly navigate to her rear seat. Those boarding the plane had no tolerance for Mom's snail's pace *(I never realized how mean people could be when they are forced to be patient with someone else)*.

When she got to her seat, she must have asked me twenty times where we were going. I was grateful when we landed in Charlotte, but the chaos continued. We decided to wait for a wheelchair assist at the airport. This allowed us to let the aircraft clear and thereby not inconvenience any of the other passengers. After about thirty minutes, the assistant arrived, and we proceeded to head directly to what we called their "new apartment."

The explosions erupted as soon as we pulled into the community parking lot.

"Where are we? I'm not staying here?"

The staff was at the entrance to greet us, and boy, they surely received a greeting they won't forget. Mom never used profanity much, but today everyone was a "dirty rotten SOB."

We quickly rolled her back to their room and tried to put a positive spin on how beautiful the room looked and told her how the staff was there to assist with anything she needed. Nothing we could say was helping. The staff even tried to intervene. She told the caregiver to "get the hell out."

The next thing I knew, Mom had gotten ahold of Dad's coat and was physically beating on his chest, screaming, "How could you do this to me? I want to go home," and several other more colorful adjectives. Dad was screaming at her to shut up. It was mortifying.

Dad was not well himself, so this beating was exceptionally upsetting. I broke it up and asked Mom to please try to control herself. Now I became the focus of all her anger. She threw her purse at me, grabbed the pillows off the bed, and threw them across the room.

"I hate you. You're a dirty rotten SOB. You've wanted to take my house and all our money for years. You're nothing more than a miserable manipulative bastard."

I left the room and just broke out in tears. The staff tried to comfort me as best they could, but my heart was broken.

They suggested I leave and come back again tomorrow. So we did.

Bill and I returned the next day with the children. I let the kids go in first, and initially, Mom didn't recognize them. Dad was thrilled to see them, but he clearly wasn't feeling very well. He complained of a stomach ache and said they didn't get much sleep the night before. I later found out that Mom kept him awake all night with her relentless harping.

The minute I walked in the door, the hateful remarks started flying again.

"Get us the —— out of here. This place is just like a prison. They won't even feed us. Who's paying for this? I'm leaving. I will find a way out, and I'm going back to my own house. You're an asshole. I wish you were never born. If you never interfered in our lives, we wouldn't be in this horrible mess."

My children overheard this cruelty, and our son immediately tried to take Grandma for a spin in her wheelchair. He was next in line to receive Mom's wrath. After being called several unsavory names himself, our son returned Grandma to the room and encouraged us all to leave.

Once again, my heart was crushed, and now my children were having to endure this too. Surprisingly, our children were intuitive enough to recognize that it was just Mom's illness and tried to encourage me to stop taking her words personally. Obviously, much easier said than done.

The children were home for a fall break from college, so we left the assisted living together and tried to grab some lunch. My nerves were shot. I kept trying to fight back the tears and did not eat a bite of my meal.

We waited a couple of days to return for a visit. We called the community frequently to get updates on their progress. Unfortunately, not much had changed. The physician group that picked up Mom's care in Charlotte recommended some medication to calm Mom's behaviors. Realizing something had to be done, I agreed.

The next visit was less violent but still full of criticism and accusations. Dad was visibly ill at this point in time. He was still wearing the same clothes he had traveled in and could barely hold up his head. I feared his cancer was worsening. We arranged for a visit to the nearby veteran's hospital for a checkup.

Later that afternoon, I received a call from the assisted living community advising that they had a flu outbreak and that the building was going to be closed to all visitors for at least the next seven to ten days. All residents were restricted to their rooms.

During that time, the facility lost Dad's dentures, and Mom grew increasingly more irritating to Dad. The staff reconfigured the one-bedroom suite to a two-bedroom layout in an effort to keep Mom from bothering Dad. He needed to rest, and she was relentless in disturbing him.

Once the building reopened, we returned for a visit to find Dad noticeably thinner, much weaker, and now unable to eat any solid foods because his teeth were missing. The facility offered no solution and claimed no responsibility for the missing dentures. They simply suggested I file an insurance claim to see if I might be able to get some assistance with replacing them. I was furious.

I looked into replacing the dentures. Not only was I facing a steep bill but also up to a three-month wait. Of course, there was no insurance coverage either.

We brought Mom and Dad to our home for Thanksgiving, and Dad had all he could do to get across the living room into the recliner. He spent his entire day in that chair. Mom enjoyed the meal but made it really clear that after dinner, I was to take her back to Buffalo. The other painful portion of this situation was to hear Mom openly criticize Dad for his "laziness." We told her he was very sick, and she showed no compassion at all. It was so difficult to hear. Dad had learned to cope by simply tuning out everything she had to say, but we could not.

When it was time to return to the assisted living community, we had to lie to Mom that we were going back to Buffalo to get her in the car. Once loaded, she was all smiles until she recognized our destination.

The children went back to college, and we limped through the weeks approaching Christmas. It was tough to manifest my traditional Christmas spirit. The pressure of the holidays, work, and my parents were taking its toll on me. My anxiety attacks began to return and were happening more frequently. I would get short of breath, my heart would start racing, and then I would break out in a sweat in the middle of the night. Medication was helpful but clearly not enough. Bill insisted I visit my doctor once again. This time, he sent me to a psychiatrist. It was determined that I needed to take a medical leave of absence from work for the next ninety days. My acute anxiety was affecting my blood pressure, cardiac performance, and ability to get adequate sleep. Now my own health was being affected, and I was frightened.

I stepped into short-term disability leave in mid-December and swear I slept for at least the first two weeks. Being away from work gave me the energy to rest and still prepare for Christmas. It turned out to be a wonderful Christmas together despite the continued displeasure that Mom exuded.

I chose not to tell my parents about my condition and continued to visit two to three times a week. I got Dad to the veteran's hospital in January only to find out that his kidney cancer had progressed into his bladder. I also learned he had an aortic aneurysm that was potentially lethal.

After this diagnosis, I discussed the need to get affairs in order. We needed to get his power of attorney as well as his final will and testament updated. He agreed, and we made arrangements to designate me as the durable power of attorney for all their affairs. Bill and I drove Dad to the attorney's office that day, and he could barely walk.

A few weeks later, Dad pulled my husband, Bill, to his bedside during one of our visits and begged him to "please take Mom somewhere…anywhere." She was keeping him from sleeping, and he couldn't listen to the nagging any longer. Bill and I made the decision that evening to have Mom come and live with us.

We lived in a three-story row house at the time and knew Mom would not be able to manage the stairs. We developed a plan to give her our master bedroom (on the first floor), and we moved up to the guest room on the second floor. This meant Bill and I were now going to swap our king-size bed for two twin beds. We had to place a baby gate on the stairs to keep Mom safe.

We brought Mom home within the next week. She was delighted to get out of that "horrible place" and really had no concern for Dad or his well-being. It was impossible for me to understand how anyone could be married for sixty-two years and demonstrate such blatant disregard for their spouse. I guess that is one of the many things I will never understand about dementia.

16

Time To Liquidate

Dad's health continued to decline, and it became clear that my parents were never going to be able to return to the home they loved so dearly.

I knew the home needed a lot of TLC before it would be ready to place on the market, so I made arrangements to meet with a recommended realtor in Buffalo. I flew back (once again), and we toured the property together. We discussed the laundry list of improvements that would need to take place, and she gave me her analysis of the estimated home value.

If we put on a new roof and renovated the kitchen and half bath, she felt like the home would easily sell for $185,000. This was more than I expected, but I had no idea what the renovation costs would turn out to be.

She provided recommendations for both a roofing company and a general renovation contractor. I took her recommendation and returned to Charlotte.

The contractors provided their estimates and timelines, but, of course, not much roofing could be done in the midst of a Buffalo winter. The roof got scheduled for the first break in the weather, and the interior renovations began within four weeks.

As in any renovation work, the actual costs exceeded the initial estimates, and the timeline took longer than expected. We finally got the final sign-off from the building inspector three weeks late and ended up spending $45,000 on the project. This was a huge risk as Mom and Dad had essentially everything they owned tied up in this home. It was imperative that we sell the home at the forecasted $185,000.

Once the renovations were complete, it was time to begin the process of cleaning out over sixty years of "collected clutter." My initial quest was to find their marriage certificate and military discharge papers, as I needed them to file for their veteran's benefits.

By now, I had exhausted all remaining time off from work, so I decided to give myself one weekend to attempt to clean out the house. Needless to say, I didn't even put a small dent in the work that needed to be done.

Dad loved to "tinker" in the garage, so he had an elaborate set of tools, and God knows how many bundles of scrap wood stuffed in every nook and cranny. I'm not sure what he was planning to build, but he had enough wood to build a small fort.

He also loved to read, and as his dementia progressed, his collection of newspaper and magazine articles grew exponentially. The stacks of papers were across his desk, stuffed in the file cabinet, and strewn across the floor. He started writing notes to himself, and I found them everywhere.

Mom kept every piece of kitchenware she ever owned. The kitchen had multiple sets of pots, pans, dishes, and silverware. She also loved to decorate. As a child, I remember the house is decked out for every holiday. All the decorations were stored away and had not been touched in ten years or more.

I remember standing in the kitchen, looking at the rest of the house, thinking, *There is no way I am ever going to clean this place out.* I did find their marriage license and military discharge paperwork after about ten hours of sifting through boxes of old photos and stacks of files. This felt like a significant victory at the moment!

The next morning, I made four trips to Goodwill with an assortment of household items and realized it was time to call in some reinforcements if I was ever going to complete this monumental undertaking. It was time to catch another flight home and begin my next plan of attack.

17

The Estate Sale

No. 12 "Stand in Faith" by Danny Gokey

Bill and I were anxious to get the newly renovated home on the market, so we crafted a plan to take a five-day trip back to Buffalo to complete the clean out and execute an estate sale.

I contacted companies that would provide clean out services, but their pricing was way too high. I attempted to hire some estate sale professionals only to find that their expertise came at a cost of 40 percent of all proceeds. Knowing that Mom and Dad needed every dime to continue their care, Bill and I decided to tackle things ourselves.

We set the date for our trip, and I began running an ad in the Buffalo News for our estate sale. We arrived on a Tuesday, and the sale was set for the following Saturday, 8:00 a.m. to 2:00 p.m.

When we arrived, I immediately placed the estate sale signs I had made on all the key roadways leading to the house. Once the signs were placed, we started filling the rental car with items for Goodwill. I lost count of how many trips we made, but I'm sure it averaged ten to twelve trips per day.

Bill took on the challenge of sifting through Dad's papers to find anything that looked important (financial, legal, or otherwise).

He found the original mortgage for the home, dated 1960, for a whopping $18,000.

I sorted through family pictures, jewelry, and collectibles for any keepsake items. By Thursday night, we were both exhausted and hadn't even priced anything for the pending estate sale. It was panic time!

The phone started ringing early Friday morning with estate shoppers wanting early preview access or questioning about tools, jewelry, antiques, etc. We were overwhelmed, to say the least.

We stopped answering the phone and decided to focus on the interior of the home and left the garage and attic alone. We pulled items out of storage and put them on the floors, counters, and tables. Nothing was priced.

We finally gave up around midnight on Friday night and woke up to people ringing the doorbell and peering in the windows at 6:30 a.m.

It was a crisp February morning, about 28 degrees, in Buffalo. It had snowed the night before, and cars were lined up on both sides of the street in front of the house. We had placed some trash bags out by the street, and people were rummaging through the trash bags.

Bill got dressed and advised the crowd that we would open at 8:00 a.m. as planned. He proceeded to communicate that we would be allowing only eight people in the house at one time, and everyone needed to enter and exit through the front door. It was a great plan but didn't really work out so well.

We determined that Bill would handle the door, and I would host shoppers inside. When we opened the door, the first group of shoppers headed in multiple directions. Because items were not priced, multiple people were making offers and often competing with one another for items. I ended up taking people's best offer on items, and I know I let many things go at unusually low prices.

We wanted all the traffic to flow through the front door to control the number of people in the home, but shoppers ended up exiting through the garage door and letting other shoppers in unsupervised. It was complete chaos. At one point, I looked out the window to see someone driving down the middle of the snow-laden street on my dad's riding lawnmower (*I was just hoping that Bill had sold it to him because I knew I didn't*).

A restoration furniture company came in and offered to buy many of the larger furniture items. Much of Mom's furniture was purchased in the 1960s, so the popularity of the "retro" design drew a significant amount of attention. The furniture resale company put sold tags on the furniture they wanted without telling us. This caused quite a stir among other interested buyers.

Everyone had to make their own arrangements to remove their purchases from the property, but this furniture company marked the items they wanted, gave me their card, and said they would be back to pay for the items and pick everything up. I had several items that people were bidding on in the midst of getting the itemization. It was awful.

It was about 4:00 p.m. when the last furniture pickup was complete, and we finally sat down for a moment. We had nowhere to sleep that night (as all the beds were sold), so we went to a nearby hotel and literally passed out.

In all the turmoil, I had forgotten to make arrangements for the final pickup of any items we did not sell. Luckily, a neighbor offered to take care of it for us. He had a big pickup truck, so his plan was to take all the wood to a salvage yard and a few cents or pounds. It was a blessing to us, as we were completely exhausted and had to fly out the very next day.

We took a final walk through the house on Sunday morning, and I can still remember how sad I felt when the "little house" that Mom and Dad loved so dearly was torn apart and empty. The childhood memories of the only home I knew growing up came flashing through my mind. It left a big hole in my heart. I closed the door behind me, and we headed for the airport.

I arranged for a housekeeping service to get the home ready to list, and it was on the market later that week.

18

Losing Dad

No. 13 "The Other Side" by Colton Dixon

Mom had been living with us for about six weeks when I got a call in the middle of the night that Dad had passed. I remember sitting up in bed and feeling essentially paralyzed. I threw my clothes on and didn't really recall the drive to his assisted living community.

When I arrived, the staff walked me to his room, where he was lying peacefully in his bed. I was shaking to the point that I felt unsteady on my feet. Tears poured down my face as I grabbed his cold hand and prayed. I apologized for not being with him when he passed. I told him I hoped I made the right decisions for both him and Mom. I thanked him for all he had done for me throughout my life. I kissed his forehead and whispered, "I love you."

I experienced loss that night like I had never felt before. Even though I knew he was sick and his overall health was declining, you're never quite prepared for the end.

Dad had not selected a funeral home and had not made any final arrangements. I took the facility's recommendation on a local funeral home. I waited until the mortuary representative arrived and watched them as they draped an American flag over his body and placed him in the hearse. Everything seemed to move in slow motion. Once they drove away, I went to the car to return home but found myself just sitting in dark silence in the parking lot.

I was certain that breaking the news of Dad's passing would be devastating to Mom, but I could not have been more wrong. I sat across from her at the breakfast table the next morning, held her hand, and softly said, "I have some bad news to share."

With tears in my eyes, I told her the news.

She was quiet for about ten seconds and said, "Well, that's too bad."

Then she matter-of-factly asked me if I wanted more banana bread. I was stunned! I thought perhaps she was in shock and things would register later, but her reaction remained consistent up to and including his memorial service.

Later that day, I had to meet with the funeral home. I did not know much about Dad's final wishes, but I did know that he wanted to be cremated. We didn't have any family nearby, and all of Dad's childhood family had passed, with the exception of a few distant cousins, whom I had no idea how to reach.

I notified my closest cousin (on my mom's side of the family) and placed a notice of Dad's passing and funeral arrangements in the Buffalo News.

His service was held at the funeral home with full military honors. Both Bill and I spoke at the funeral, but it was a very small group in attendance. The uniformed service members folded a burial flag and presented it to Mom while others played Taps in the back of the service. Mom sat in the front row, emotionless. I was a tearful mess.

On the way home, Mom's only comment was, "That was nice." After the service, we had a reception at our home that was fully catered. Some friends and neighbors dropped by, and in the midst of their visit, Mom blurts out, "What's all the fuss? I'm hungry. Let's eat."

The kindest words I heard her say were to my cousin, whom she adored.

I overheard, "The old man was a pretty good egg, I guess." It almost felt like she was talking about some stranger. I remember thinking how hurt Dad would have been to hear her speak of him in such a run-of-the-mill fashion.

19

At Home with Mom

No. 14 "Overcomer" by Mandisa

Mom's dementia continued to progress in the weeks following Dad's death. She now required round-the-clock care and was no longer able to dress or toilette herself. She used a walker to ambulate and was consistently waking up throughout the night.

She would ask, "Where is your father? When can I go back to Buffalo? Why am I here?" She would often wake the entire house up when she would head down the hallway banging her walker on the floor. She let the dogs out multiple times, and the only thing that kept them from running away was our invisible fence. We got to know the police department quite well after she set off the house alarm several times.

We hired an in-home caregiver service during work hours, but she would treat them horribly. "Get her the —— out of here. I don't need any —— help!" would be her consistent response when they would arrive at the door. She would hide from the caregiver throughout the day and even lock herself in her bedroom.

Her mood swings were as unpredictable as the wind. One morning, she would think Bill was her boyfriend or best friend. The next morning, he might be a stranger in the house.

Mom used to try to help in the kitchen, and I would continually find the dog dishes where the mixing bowls are stored and cooking utensils in the oven or refrigerator.

She would take meats out of the freezer and place them in the pantry to thaw. We would find cereal, chips, and cookies all stored in the same Tupperware containers.

Over time, I learned to "roll" with these harmless annoyances until, one night, the risk became too high. Our daughter was home from college when she woke up one morning with Grandma hovering over her bed on the second floor. She had removed the baby gate at the bottom of the stairs and managed to maneuver her way upstairs in the middle of the night. Our daughter woke up startled, and Mom had no idea where she was.

Bill and I came running out of our new bedroom (also on the second floor) and realized immediately that it was no longer safe for Mom to stay in our home. If she had tried to head down the stairs on her own, she would have fallen for sure. A fall like that could have killed her.

20

Memory Care

Here we go again, searching for another senior care facility. Now I had to learn about memory care services. I had no idea what I was looking for, but I had my Google list, and off I went.

I quickly learned that memory care communities are essentially "locked down" extensions of assisted living facilities. It was also abundantly obvious that memory care residents require a much higher level of care too. It took some adjustment to the fact that many had very limited verbal skills, and many were wheelchair-bound.

I knew after visiting my first two facilities that this was going to be the toughest transition yet.

I ended up choosing a community close to our home that was in the middle range on pricing. Memory care was clearly going to be more expensive. Once the decision was made and the timeline in place, we began the task of trying to get Mom excited about what we called her "new apartment."

I made several trips to the community to decorate the room for her. We hung drapery, her favorite family pictures, and put familiar bedding on her new bed. I was fooling myself to think it mattered, and as expected, she threw a fit when I brought her in for the first time. What I didn't anticipate was her cruelty to the other residents. "Look at these people, they can't speak, they're drooling, wandering all over the place. Do you think I'm crazy or something?" were her first remarks. She shared her thoughts for all to hear as well. I was mortified!

I quickly shuffled her into her room and tried to direct her attention to the nice decor. I started to unpack her things and place them in the dresser, and she promptly pulled everything out of the dresser and put it back in her suitcase. I left the suitcase on her bed and escorted her to dinner in the dining room. She started complaining about the food, pulled the hamburger out of the bun, and started banging it on the table.

"Would you eat this crap?" she asked.

The staff was watching my struggle and swooped in to try to diffuse the situation. They told me to slip out and come back tomorrow, so I did.

The house was peaceful that evening, but my guilt was all-consuming. I called to check on her and was told she was adjusting well. I knew that was only a half-truth at best. The staff kept assuring me they were fully prepared to deal with her behaviors.

I stopped by after work almost every day for the first couple of weeks. I would take her outside (weather permitting), and I would try to field the same questions multiple times. "When am I going home? Why did you make me come here?" As time went on, the comments got meaner. "They are terribly mean to me here? This is an awful place. The people are crazy. They are stealing all my stuff? I hate you so much. You're evil" were just some of the remarks that left lasting scars. These visits would often end in tears for me. I can remember sitting in the car in the parking lot, just sobbing.

The staff suggested I begin to cut back on the frequency of my visits. I shifted to three times per week. I would always make a point of bringing an ice cream sundae, donuts, a milkshake, or some kind of sweet treat to brighten her day. I can still see how her face would light up for a sweet treat. She would enjoy the treat and the visit for a short time and then revert back to her displeasure. I learned not to stay long enough to let it get too hurtful.

Mom's behaviors continued to heighten, and after she got in a fight with another resident, I received a call from the staff to come in for a care plan review. During this meeting, the nurse recommended we place Mom on some behavior medications in an attempt to curb some of her outbursts. I agreed, of course. What I didn't know was what effect it was going to have on her.

I went to visit the next time, and she was propped up in a chair, sleeping with her mouth gaping open. It took a few tries to get her to wake up, and when she came around, she was only halfway there. Her speech was slurred, and all she wanted to do was go back to sleep. Needless to say, I was not happy about the medication regimen the community had implemented. I called a meeting with the clinical team, and they agreed to try another medication.

21

Hip No. 2

No. 15 "God's Not Done with You" by Tauren Wells

The new medication seemed to be calming her down versus completely knocking her out, so I agreed to continue with this secondary solution. I did notice that she was much more unsteady on her feet and seemed to have lost her once-healthy appetite. The staff assured me it was a temporary side effect.

Mom had been in this memory care community for about six weeks when I received a call that she had fallen. EMS was transporting her to the hospital, and they suspected she had fractured her other hip. Evidently, she tried to walk across her room without her walker and slipped in the bathroom.

Sure enough, she was heading to surgery when I arrived at the hospital. Another hip replacement with extended recovery ahead. I started wondering how much more hardship she would be able to take.

I met her in the recovery room at the hospital, and she had absolutely no idea what had happened. No recollection of the fall or the surgery. Although she was in a good deal of pain, she was released after three days and cleared for therapy within her memory care community. This is usually not the case after a major surgery like this, but Mom's dementia had progressed to the point where her physicians felt like she would be best suited for recovery in a memory care facility. She had daily rehabilitation therapy for the next few weeks.

It didn't take the therapy team long to advise that Mom was not cooperating. She showed no interest in recovering and was clearly demonstrating signs of depression. We decided to adjust her medication once again to see if we might be able to inspire some desire.

At this point, Mom is spending most of her days in a wheelchair. She can bear enough weight to stand and pivot for the staff, but it is not likely that she will ever walk again. I would visit and take her for a rollout to the courtyard gazebo to enjoy the sunshine, flowers, and fresh air. This was clearly something she enjoyed immensely. I felt grateful that I could bring her that small joy.

Strangely enough, these days with Mom were among the most precious to me. She was more accepting of her limitations and grew more appreciative of all the care surrounding her. She no longer recognized Bill and the children when they would visit, but she would always react to me.

Sometimes I was her mom. Other times I might be a sister, cousin, or old friend. The good news is that she was almost always glad to have a visit.

We shared many ice cream sundaes, milkshakes, chocolates, and pastry items over the next few weeks. Although she wasn't completely aware of who I was, I know my visits brought her joy. One of my most treasured conversations with Mom happened one day when we were sitting in the gazebo. A butterfly was flitting around us, and she noticed how beautiful it was. I made the comment that some believe that when a butterfly stops by to visit, it is a sign that a loved one that has passed wants to get your attention. She laughed, and she immediately said it must be her sister (who had recently passed). She spoke about her sister and began to tell stories about her childhood.

"I had four brothers and sisters, you know. I was the middle of all the children and the first girl. I was always my Dad's favorite. I was also the troublemaker in the family, you know. I didn't go to college because I wanted to be an airline stewardess. I loved that job and got to travel all over the world. After that, I decided to join the navy because that's where all the eligible men were," she said with a big grin on her face.

She went on to say that her navy job was as a secretary to the naval officers. It was great fun. During that time, she was approached by a naval magazine to be a model. She was very flattered by this invitation.

Just as suddenly as the stories began, she slipped into silence. We sat in silence for a few minutes, but the butterfly kept flirting with her. I had been wanting to ask Mom a faith-related question for way too long now, so I took advantage of this opportunity. I shared the butterfly story with her again and proceeded to ask her if she believed in heaven. She had never been much of a religious person over the years, so as it was clear her time on this earth may be over soon, I wanted to know if she believed in Jesus and life after death. I remember being so nervous to get her to openly state her beliefs. I could feel my heart beating out of my chest, but it was like God Himself wanted me to proceed. She paused for a few moments and said, "Of course I do!"

I felt such happiness and relief. This was the first time I knew for sure that she was a believer. It brought me so much comfort. We never spoke of it again, but now I knew and she had verbalized what I believe was the most important statement a person can make. I thanked God when I got to the car that afternoon because I believe He orchestrated that opportunity for us.

22

Finally Home

No. 16 "Tell Your Heart to Beat Again" by Danny Gokey

Over the next few weeks, Mom grew increasingly weaker. She was spending more and more time in bed and grew less interested in my visits. I was sad when I couldn't get her to go outside with me and even more heartbroken when the ice cream and other treats I brought would no longer inspire a big smile!

Our conversations diminished to one or two sentences at best. I would sit for hours and just hold her hand. I felt helpless to be able to do anything further for her.

I knew she was losing her will to live when she said to me one day, "Will you please just let me die? Why won't all of you just let me die?"

As you can imagine, I had no idea how to respond, so I simply said something like, "That's nonsense, don't talk like that." That was obviously the wrong answer, but it was the only one I could come up with at the time.

The staff advised that it was probably time for me to engage with a hospice team. Of course, I had no idea what wonderful services a hospice team could provide because I was like most people who think of hospice as a surrender to death. I met with the recommended hospice team, and they could not have been more kind, comforting, and supportive. Once they explained their services, I knew it was the right next step in Mom's care.

We completed another round of intense paperwork, and they began caring for Mom right away. They eliminated most of Mom's medications and focused on keeping her as comfortable as possible. These medication changes gave me the gift of several moments of crystal clear clarity with her. She told me how I was her angel over the last few years. She wanted me to know that she loved me very much. She was never one to say much about her feelings, so these moments are permanently engraved in my heart.

She had stopped eating and drinking at this point in her journey, and she spent most of her day in the fetal position in her bed. I knew her time with us was limited.

I was still having to travel for work and received a call from the hospice team while I was out of town. They advised me that we didn't have much time left and that I should come home as soon as possible.

My flight was later that day, and I went straight to the facility as soon as my plane hit the ground. I honestly don't remember the drive, but I do remember walking into Mom's room with the hospice nurse by her side. The nurse told me that Mom was hanging on to wait for me. All her vital signs were poor, but she felt like Mom was waiting for me to say goodbye. She left the room, and I knelt by her bed, held her hand, and wept. I thought about all the things she had done for me in my lifetime. All the times she was there to encourage me. She had been like the sister I never had and probably knew me better than anyone. All the hurt, hardship, and unpleasantries had faded away.

I remember brushing my hand across her cheek and telling her, "I love you, Mom. It's okay for you to go. I am grateful you allowed me to have this moment with you to say goodbye." I took another thirty minutes or so to get myself together, and then I headed home to my family. It was a terribly sad evening for all of us.

That evening, I received a call from the hospice team to advise that Mom had passed in her sleep. My heart was broken, but her journey was finally over. She was finally home.

Parents have an unmatched, irreplaceable impact on our lives. They are our first teachers, our biggest fans, our counselors, disciplinarians, best friends, and providers. No one can ever fill the void that they leave behind when their life with us comes to an end, but I try (even now) to remember what an amazing gift they were to me and know I will see them again one day.

Lessons Learned

Now that you've read my story, love and loss are probably pretty clear, so I wanted to complete my message to you by sharing what I have learned.

I believe every experience we encounter is intended to teach us something. I also am convinced that these "lessons learned" are of greater value when they are shared.

So here is a summary of what I have learned from this ten-year dementia journey:

1. Ordinary Life

    Had I known more about the early signs of dementia, I would have taken the changes I noticed in Mom and Dad's behavior more seriously instead of simply attributing it to old age (weight loss, repeating questions and stories, and short tempers).

    I would have gotten less annoyed when the dishes were all put away in the wrong places or the socks that Mom just matched were a "hot mess." I would have understood that she was just trying to be helpful and feel valued.

2. Signs

    People suffering from dementia will often begin to neglect many of the things they used to hold in high regard (personal hygiene, housekeeping, home maintenance, and hobbies). The things they used to love to do may fade away. If I knew these changes were caused by the onset of dementia, I would have been less critical and more understanding.

I would have taken action to get important documents like the will, power of attorney, and final wishes in order while they were still able to provide clear responses. I would have made sure I knew where all the legal documents were located, so I wouldn't have to hunt for them later *(Medicare cards, supplemental health policies, homeowner, auto, life insurance, military discharge papers, marriage certificate, social security cards, property deed, safety deposit box details, investments, and banking information).*

I would have been more courageous regarding the tasks that I was able to address for them. Rather than asking for permission, I would have simply hired someone to plow the driveway, mow the lawn, and pick up groceries. I would position these services as a gift from me rather than something I thought they needed.

I realize now that it wasn't the task that led to the negative response, and it was their rejection of the fact that they needed help in those areas.

3.   Cover-Up

I would have been less surprised by Mom and Dad's cover-up on important incidents if I understood that keeping things from me was there way of hiding the fact that mistakes were being made that they were embarrassed about. Dementia patients realize something is wrong but will try to cover it up for as long as they possibly can.

If I suspected they would keep things from me, I would have arranged to be more connected to dad's physicians at the Veteran's Hospital. I would have made sure he added me to the authorized communication list for all his medical information. I would have checked in with them more frequently and paid for a neighbor or friend to do some random drop-ins for me.

Knowing that dementia affects the person's ability to comprehend situations, I would have been more patient when I had to explain the insurance claim process fifteen times after Dad's car accident. I would have broken things down into simple steps, written them out for him, and then reviewed them.

I would have remained calmer during those times when tension ran high if I knew that the arguing and lashing out were largely driven by the frustration that comes with dementia. I would have been more sensitive to the fact that their entire world (as they knew it) is changing, and they cannot control what is happening.

4. On the Road

Driving is one of the most difficult situations to overcome for dementia patients. Taking the keys away is like taking their freedom away. Calling on the services of the local police department might help. If an officer of the law communicates the need to stop driving, it will be much more powerful than anything you or I might say.

I should have anticipated that the time would come when I would need all of their medical, homeowners, and auto insurance information. This would have made processing all claims much easier.

If I were local, I would have arranged to do all the transporting. I should have considered paying a neighbor or friend to take them on errands. I didn't realize the importance of setting these arrangements up early in the dementia process. Trust is everything, and those with dementia are increasingly afraid of strangers. If they don't develop a friend (or circle of friends) that they trust early, they will likely never let anyone help.

5. First Few Swings and Being the Punching Bag

I realize now that a person with dementia is always right. There is absolutely no value in arguing with them. I would not have argued as much. I would have learned to agree and move to the next subject.

Realizing that people dealing with dementia are experiencing a form of brain failure that often eliminates all social filters. I would not have been as mortified as I was when Mom had terrible things to say about Dad or others. I would have understood that her mood swings, outbursts, and social skills were all related to her dementia and would have tried to take them less personally.

I would not have wasted time listing the things I was concerned about because they were both incapable of identifying the things I was seeing. I would have just taken action in a roundabout, unthreatening way.

I have since learned about the power of redirection. If I had been exposed to this skill during this journey, I could have eliminated a lot of arguments, hurt feelings, and frustration.

I would not have even considered asking them to travel to visit. I now realize how stressful that was for them. Dementia affects all their senses as well as their balance. Asking them to navigate a busy airport, go through security, and connect flights was way too much to ask.

6. I'm Scared and Everybody's Angry

I wish I would have been able to understand more about the world through their eyes during this time. It would have made me more patient and less quick to criticize. Although it was natural for me to be scared, I think I spent so much time with my worries that I never saw their fear.

I should have found help and support sooner. I've learned that dementia is a struggle that should not be tackled alone.

7. Taking Its Toll

I've learned that stress is no joke. I learned the hard way that even though you think you've got this, the stress will bring you to your knees if you are not careful.

Stress is not the impact of a single incident, trauma, or conflict. It is that slow drip that builds up over time until it becomes too much for your mind and body to bear. Then you break.

Take care of yourself during any dementia journey. Get a circle of people that can lend a hand, give you good information, and simply support you. Prayer is a great source of strength too.

8. The Fall

Dementia impacts judgment. It makes it difficult to determine right from wrong and safe from unsafe. When we are unable to make a clear and confident decision, we often make the wrong one. Dad didn't mean to let Mom lay on the floor for multiple days, but he was just unable to make a sound decision, so he did nothing.

I learned not to take the recommendation for therapy and assisted living from the first hospital social worker that happens to come across my path. Do your research. Check reviews. Visit the facilities. Understand all the costs and services. Meet with the staff before making any decisions.

9. The Storm and The Tsunami

Changing a dementia patient's environment and routine can be devastating. It will likely accelerate their dementia. You must be heavily involved in any change that takes place.

Seniors need a strong advocate in today's senior living world. They need someone to follow up, take action, and consistently inquire on their behalf.

Do not expect the facility staff to do this for you. They are well intended but will never have the ability to singularly focus on your loved one.

10. No More Choices

This was when I learned about something called the "therapeutic fib." I didn't know what it was at the time, but it can be a very effective tool in your dementia management toolbox. For the most part, I recommend that you tell your loved one the truth, but when that has been consistently ineffective, a fib that might move you closer to compliance might be in order. I recognized that senior living was a necessary next step for Mom and Dad, but the costs were a barrier. I researched the veteran's aid and assistance program and found some financial assistance. It was not enough to cover the entire cost, so I embellished a little to tell Dad that the veteran's funding and Medicare would cover the cost of their assisted living. For the record, Medicare does not cover assisted living, and the veteran's program is typically paid in arrears, but it was enough to reach compliance.

I also learned to take any win in this process, even the small ones. Dad agreeing to a temporary stay in Charlotte was a step in the right direction. I knew I had financial power of attorney, so the therapeutic fib could be somewhat disguised.

11. Shopping for Assisted Living

Legwork is critical in this process. Visit the facilities in person. I suggest coming in unannounced. Speak to the residents. Watch the staff (are they happy, engaged, and polite?). Observe activities to see what attendance looks like and if the residents are engaged.

12. The Move

Plan every detail. Travel on a less-busy day. Expect resistance. Try to communicate what to expect in advance to dementia travelers. Break it down and give them only what they need to get them through the next step in the process. Bring help. Don't rush things. Allow extra time for everything. Mentally prepare for explosions.

13. Time to Liquidate

Prepare for the fact that this will take much longer than you expected. Also, try to prepare for the emotional side of the liquidation process, as there are so many memories that come up. Gathering all the family pictures is a heart-wrencher.

Research your real estate partner. Get more than one market analysis of the property. If repairs are needed, find a trusted contractor. The listing realtor I encountered gave us a market value of $185,000 for the home. This drove our decision to spend $45,000 on renovations. The home sat on the market for months and eventually sold for $115,000. Painful experience.

14. The Estate Sale

Allow yourself two to three weeks to prepare. Bring lots of help. Advertise two weeks in advance in the local paper and then use street signs a few days before the sale. Do not provide a phone number for buyers to reach you. Price everything in advance. Establish one entry and exit. Develop a process to manage the number of shoppers allowed in the home at once (suggest ten laminated cards that are given upon entry. Number must be returned to the next in line for entry). Assign one person to handle all transactions. Arrange for donation pickups (especially on the bigger items). Habitat for Humanity, Salvation Army, and others all have pickup services.

There are also services that you can hire that will handle all of this for you. They will negotiate a percentage of the gross sales as their fee.

15. Losing Dad

Dementia can steal (what we would see as normal) emotional reactions to significant events. I can honestly say that I never saw Mom shed a tear regarding Dad's passing. If I had known that dementia could have this kind of impact, I would have been less shocked at her matter-of-fact, emotionless response. I initially thought it might be her way of coping with the loss at the time of the funeral, but we got the same reaction each of the multiple times we had to tell her of his passing.

16. At Home with Mom

Expect to have the house alarms set off, the pets to get released, and the dishes to be found in the most unusual places. If in-home care is required, try to request a caregiver that is dementia trained and see if you can secure the same caregiver each visit.

If you going to live with someone with dementia, you must learn how to communicate differently (using all your senses and body language). You must also learn the skill of redirecting.

Dementia patients want to do things that have a purpose and add value to the household, so find the things they can still do to help and put them to work.

Order out for additional patience. Your whole family will need it.

17. Memory Care

A good memory care community is so much more than a secure community. The same principles apply to searching for general assisted living, but I would ask how many of the staff are certified in dementia care. Activities are critical, so be sure they are happening, and there is a high level of engagement.

Visit often. Plan your visit. Be a proactive advocate for your loved one. Stay connected to the physicians, nurses, care staff, and medications. Speak up on your loved one's behalf.

If the community doesn't like what you have to say or doesn't respond—move out. Communities are typically only a thirty-day commitment, so you are free to find a better solution at any point in the cycle.

18. Hip No. 2

Dementia is a double-edged sword in this situation. It enabled Mom to forget she went through the trauma of another hip replacement surgery, but it also lets her forget she cannot walk on that leg during the recovery process. Dementia patients at this stage need constant supervision to avoid falls.

19. Finally Home

Late-stage dementia is heartbreaking because the person you know and love appear to be gone. Many families make the determination that because their loved one has no idea who they are or may not be responsive that there is no further value in visiting. This is absolutely wrong.

It has been proven that emotional memory is the last part of the human brain to be affected by dementia. This means that even if they can no longer respond to you, they still know you are there. Your presence is felt, and it matters. I know my mom waited until I was able to get to her to say my final goodbyes before she passed. You hear this story time and again as people live out their final days. Don't miss any moment you are given to be fully present for the ones you love.

This recap is not intended to be a complete summary of things to learn during a dementia journey. Every journey is as different as the person it impacts. My hope is that you may get a few ideas that may ease your journey and comfort you along the way.

A Few Final Thoughts

God doesn't want us to go through hardships on our own, so He surrounded me with a loving family, amazing neighbors, and skilled care providers.

He gives us basic skills that help us "get by" while we're caring for dementia patients, but there is much to learn that will make the journey easier. I was never trained on what to do when Mom and Dad's dementia was at its worst, but I learned these basic tricks:

1. A person with dementia is always right, even if they are not. It never does any good for anyone to argue. Correction is not effective, so learn to "roll with it."
2. Successfully redirecting dementia patients is both an art and a skill. It's worth perfecting, however.
3. I've learned that we (as caregivers) are the ones who have to adapt because our loved ones can't. We must learn to recognize that whatever they are doing is *not* their fault. It is their cognitive disability driving their actions, words, and behaviors.

We have to change our perspective when dealing with dementia. We must learn to focus on making the best of what we have left with the ones we love that are in this fight—and not all the things they can no longer do.

I've learned that God will give you those moments of clarity with your loved one, and that will warm your heart and keep you going.

The Bible tells us that God uses the challenges and hardships in this lifetime to draw us closer to Him. He uses tough times to teach us to rely on Him completely. It is when we are at our lowest that our faith grows the most. Hardships are never fun, but they do play a part in God's story of our lives.

Lastly, and most importantly, I have learned that God has been with you (and will continue to be by your side) *through all of it*!

*****

This journey has profoundly changed my life. It has propelled me into a new career and personal mission that is solely focused on assisting seniors, their families, and their caregivers.

I have served as a director of three assisted living and four memory care communities in recent years. I have made it my personal ambition to be both a student and a teacher of the skills necessary to successfully deal with dementia.

In addition to my license to run a senior living community, I am also a nationally licensed dementia trainer through the National Council of Certified Dementia Practitioners (NCCDP). I train caregivers of all kinds (in person and online), offer support groups, provide one on one counseling, and execute memory café events in my local state of South Carolina.

I can always be reached at my website, *dealingwdementia.com*. Please visit the site and sign up for my newsletter and blog.

My greatest prayer for you is that you reach out to get the help and support you will need, whether it's through me or someone else that can help.

Keep praying. Ask our good and gracious God to strengthen your every step. He'll be there for you, guaranteed!

About the Author

In many ways, Peggy is probably a lot like you. She is a wife, mom, daughter, friend, coworker, and Christian. She is also a retired marketing executive that has been blessed to work for *(and with)* several Fortune 500 companies. In addition to her thirty-plus years of corporate experience, she launched a second career in senior care with a keen focus on dementia. Today she is running her own social impact organization called Dealing with Dementia. Her mission is to inform, train, and support families, caregivers, and patients faced with this diagnosis.

Peggy believes that every challenge or hardship we encounter across the course of our life has a greater purpose. She'll openly tell you that we are supposed to learn something from each experience and then share our learning with others. Investing in others is a core value for Peggy, and it is the driving force behind her writing and everything she does.

Today, Peggy continues to invest in others through her executive coaching, dementia training, support groups, mentoring, and public speaking. She is a huge fan of contemporary Christian music (*as you will find woven in all her books*). It's also quite possible that you may find her singing her heart out as some stoplight in South Carolina!

She has three beloved writing assistants that have been immensely supportive over the years. (Rory, Moose [both chocolate labs], and Boone, our bloodhound). When she is not working, you will likely find her playing with her beloved dogs, gardening, or sitting in her beach chair with the waves rolling over her toes.